Contents

Chapter I
The beginnings of sail

The classic picture of the first man afloat usually takes the form of a bemused looking, fur-clad, apeman inadvertently adrift on a log. The mirror-like surface of the pond is disturbed only by his hands as he thoughtfully invents paddling. From such a beginning it is tempting to draw a line of research and development through the years, to cover paddling and rowing until we reach man's supreme achievement – sailing to windward.

This of course is evident nonsense. The only mystery about the invention of sailing ships is the quite minor one of record. Sailing in fact is a natural function of anything which floats where a wind blows and that is almost everywhere. The smallest water bug uses the wind to voyage across ponds; leaves, twigs and other items of nature's detritus can do nothing but sail downwind and even the elegant swan is designed to raise a handsome

Below *An Egyptian burial boat of about 2040-1780 BC. It was built on the basis of the Dashur boat and would have been contemporary with those found at Saqquara.*

Right *A Peruvian papyrus reed boat with full sail. This type of boat is still in use in Peru and until recently was used extensively in Tasmania.*

Below *Fishermen on Lake Titicaca in Peru. The people still use their papyrus reed boats for fishing in the waters of the lake. This type of boat is very similar to those of the early Egyptians. The reeds are bundled together with regular lashings, into a long, thin hull form, in the style of a slight crescent.*

Far right *This buff decorated pot is characteristic of the Nacquara 11, i.e. the Gerzean or pre-Dynastic culture about 3300 B.C. It depicts a sailing boat of that period, with sail and oars. It was probably built of acacia and sycamore, which grow in abundance along the Nile.*

pair of running sails, when the wind serves her purpose. The biggest problem facing the first waterman might well have been how to avoid sailing too smartly away from home and all he held dear. In such a predicament you would find anyone scrabbling in the water with feet and hands, to get back to shore or poking desperately with a stick to stop the craft blowing further and further away. By the time the errant craft had blown clear of soundings, early man would have invented in some form the whole basic gamut of boating right up to the mechanical age in one ten minute span of time.

The real ingredients of development are man and materials. There is little evidence that early man, in historical times at least, was any less intelligent than ourselves. Scarcely educated and less adequately equipped certainly, but no less enterprising and no

By watching the creatures of the water, man discovers Sail

less ingenious than ourselves. Ships and boats represented the front rank of technology for centuries, in fact for all of man's days until the aeroplane. The ship was the space craft of most civilizations and it was designed and built and manned with the same calibre of intellect as nowadays plans voyages among the stars.

The past, dug up from the mud or found in museums or attics, usually looks motheaten, dusty, and worn out. The past as seen in our elders is represented by the tired and aged, giving man a natural feeling of superiority over previous generations and things. It is often difficult for us to visualize early craft when they were new, bright as buttons, clean and smart as yachts and manned by fit and intelligent youngsters.

Our first sailors, therefore, after they got over their baptisms, would quickly realise why they were so rudely propelled over the surface of the sea and no doubt as quickly noticed that they had a fair measure of control over the process. If the wind was fair they could stand up, spread their arms and furs to catch the wind and speed along. If the wind blew the wrong way then it was a question of making a low profile and looking to paddling or stick work to make progress. In no time at all we can see the fur or cloak stuck up on a stick and early man under full sail thinking no more of harnessing nature to help him in this enterprise, than he would about conservation and pollution when drinking from a stream.

Two other practical facts which affect any consideration of the beginning of sailing should also be mentioned. First is that it is not at all easy to get a boat to sail properly down wind. A normal rudderless boat will lie broadside or slightly bow into the wind and drift, very slowly, sideways. The downwind boat therefore very often steps the mast well forward to improve the self steering and always will have a rudder or some other means of directional control. The other fact is that the wind seldom blows in a constant direction and therefore any sailor would quickly experience the effects of wind blowing his craft and sails from every angle. Almost any old rag of a sail in a boat with a rudder will sail it along at right angles to the wind. Early sails, by their very simplicity, were in fact often capable of windward sailing and the only bar to the boat using this capability was the increased sideways drift as the boat is brought up towards the wind. The history and possibility of windward sailing therefore depends very much more on the development of windward working hull forms, than in rig.

Mesopotamia and Egypt, followed by the Mediterranean Sea in general, are usually credited

in European civilizations with the beginnings and development of the arts of sailing and voyaging in ships. Possibly Polynesia and the Chinese have equally good claims and by and large it is not a matter of great importance. The real interest lies in the developments in materials and know-how which brought the sailing ship from a log propelled by a fur skirt stuck on a pole, to the more complex scientific miracles of the great days of the clipper ships. Science is not exclusively applicable to test tubes and computers but is equally present in sticks and strings laced together into a pattern of logic and efficiency as beautiful and precise as any printed circuit.

It is thought that the Chinese were using flat rafts made of bamboo at about the time of the beginning of the first stone age, 4000 BC. Another of the earliest civilizations developed between the rivers Tigris and Euphrates and what may be the earliest surviving model sailing boat, dating back to 3500 BC, was dug up there at *Eridu*. It is a high sided, tub shaped vessel with pointed ends and what looks like a mast step inside. One could also believe that the brace across one end might be a helmsman's seat or even a sheet horse for the sail and that the holes in the sides are for shrouds or oars. It is really a bit of a mystery for the hull shape infers that it would most likely be a small craft

Egyptian papyrus fishing canoes, from the tomb of Chancellor Mehenkvetre. In about 2000 BC he was buried with a good collection of models, both of the papyrus boats and of early sailing ships.

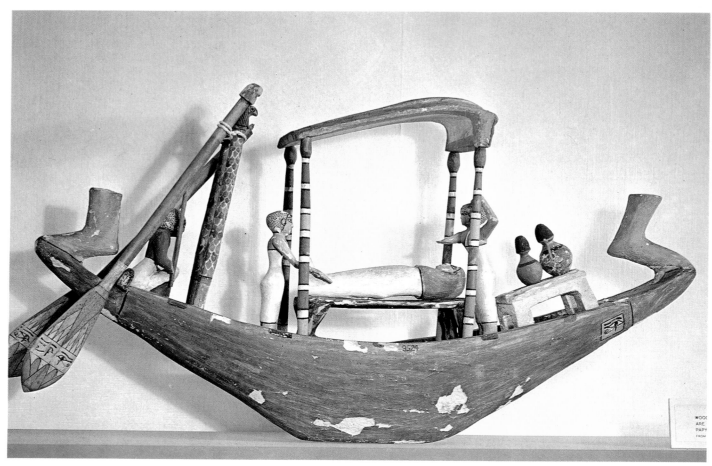

made in a basket type of construction covered with skins whereas the mast step, etc. belong rather more to a bigger vessel which might have been made of wood in a manner not seen again for a thousand years. Another explanation, which may be equally valid is that it is not a model boat at all but a candle holder, fancy dish of some sort, or even an ash tray.

The dynastic periods of Egyptian civilization have left the best traces of their early craft. Before they started, about 3400 BC, with Menes the first Pharaoh it seems likely that the Egyptians were already trading by sea with Syria and Crete, representing offshore voyages of 200 miles or so. However, the principal waterway of Egypt is the River Nile which has normally a good north wind blowing over the north-going current. The Nile boatmen could therefore blow upstream or drift downstream with only the minimum of rowing and the minimum need to develop anything other than straight down wind sailing. Egyptian boatbuilders were not so well served. To hand they had only acacia and sycamore in small trees and a great deal of papyrus reed. It is likely therefore, that the earliest Egyptian boats were essentially spool shaped bundles of reeds, much as are used to the present day in some parts of the upper Nile and in such places as Lake Titicaca in Peru, and even until recently in Tasmania. The reeds were bundled together with regular lashings into a long thin hull form in the style of a slight crescent to lift the ends out of the water. The bundle was made as wide as possible for stability and an extra bundle was put on top so that the crew and cargo rode reasonably dry. One end at least was looped heavily back and secured with stout lashing in the form of a bow string, to give a quite sophisticated method of pre-tensioning the hull against sag when loaded.

Reed vessels, like those of Ancient Egypt are still used in Peru

Thor Heyerdahl in his experiments with seagoing reed rafts, believed that this also allowed a form of articulation to occur when the reed boat was working heavily in heavy seas.

Southern Egyptian archaeologists have found hundreds of pictures of boats drawn it is thought about 2900 BC. These show the typical spool-shaped hulls of reed boats and some show a simple squaresail of apparently modest size, set well forward. These are important as being about the earliest pictures of boats under sail so far discovered. The stem rears up ahead of the sail to a great height with an indication at the top of what may be leads for yard braces and following the same theme there appear to be a pair of outriggers set low on the hull where nowadays one would fit catheads for the bowlines. Both of which, if correctly interpreted, infer that the sail was braced round to suit the wind direction. On the other hand the mast is shown right forward which would indicate a ship used for downwind sailing only.

Reliefs dating from about 2800 BC show workmen in the act of binding up a papyrus boat and also

apparently building a boat of wood, and it seems that about this time the Egyptians were becoming skilful in planking hulls from the short planks of the indigenous trees. From models and from excavations of pits made for real ships, Egyptian vessels of this period appear to be about as big as 70 feet in length with a beam of 17 or 18 feet in a wide, flat spoon form. However, the most impressive relics were found in pits close to the pyramid of *Cheops* and dating back to about 2700 BC. A number of vessels were found, all in pieces but excellently preserved. They included the remains of at least one complete ship, dismantled but placed ready for reconstruction, and this is now being rebuilt. She is 140 feet long and has a beam of nearly 20 feet and is said to be both graceful and sturdy. The keel-less bottom

The tombs of Egypt reveal the secrets of Egyptian sailing ships

planking starts with three cedar boards about 6 inches thick down the centre, with other boards edge fastened to them with acacia treenails (wood pegs) glued into place. In addition, the planks are lashed together inside through holes drilled in them, using ropes of halfa grass and then are caulked with papyrus. The shell appears to be further reinforced with some interior frames added after completion of the hull. The timber is Lebanon cedar and the two largest parts are over 80 feet long and nearly 30 inches square. These are longitudinal stiffeners fitted under the deck near to the sides of the vessel.

Cedar was very important to the Egyptians as a boat building material and hieroglyphics show that in 2650 BC Pharaoh Snefru sent no less than forty ships to Byblos to buy cedar. Reliefs dating from 2550 BC show an expedition which Pharaoh Sahure sent to Syria and these show very much the same kind of ships. Built from relatively short blocks of timber, without any real keel, the ships were braced and secured with rope lashings very much of the same style that was used for the papyrus reed boats. The hull was girdled with one or more stout ropes and was further braced in the bowstring manner with a stout rope truss in effect knotted around each end of the hull and braced off the deck on fork-ended poles. These ships had high stem and stern posts but these appear to have no real structural significance and may be no more than ancestral styling retained because they made a convenient leaning post for the lookouts and for decoration.

The sailing equipment was quite interesting consisting of a bipod mast with an apparently tall squaresail set on a yard at the top and probably loose footed at the bottom. The mast is very well equipped with backstays but with only a single forestay, indicating that it normally worked with the wind aft. A feature of most Egyptian ships is the multiplicity of steering oars and in this case three are shown, possibly to be matched by three on the other side of the stern. The alternative method of propulsion is shown as oars which have taken over from paddles with the size of the craft to be propelled.

Left This Egyptian model of about 2000 BC shows in more detail the rigging and steering mechanisms of these early sailing ships. These models and remains found in other parts of the world give us a fairly clear picture of the chronological order of the development of the sailing ship.

11

The Cairo Museum has two actual boats of the XII dynasty about 2000 BC and others have been excavated at *Saqqara*. It was part of the beliefs of the time that a boat was necessary to transport the dead on their first trip and therefore boats were buried as a normal part of tomb furniture. The Saqqara boats, it is thought, were actually used to transport the dead across the Nile. One of the boats is about 33 feet long with about 8 feet beam. It is constructed, like the other Egyptian style of ships, without a constructional keel but with a line of carefully fitted centreline planks to which small wood blocks are pinned to complete the planking. Deck beams are fitted projecting through the side planking and secured with a heavy top strake.

A fine collection of model ships was found in Mehenkvetre's tomb

Pharaoh Mentuhotep, who reigned about 2000 BC, had a chancellor called Mehenkvetre who was buried with a good collection of models. One shows a rather refined version of the papyrus boat with the bow and stern covered with a fine decorative leather cover and a painted washboard fitted each side of the centrebody. More interesting perhaps are the models of sailing ships. One of these shows a pole mast counterweighted with a stone to allow it to be raised and dropped with ease. Both the sailing models had the masts just forward of amidships fitted with a wide squaresail. The yard at the top is fitted with three lifts a side while the lower yard at the foot of the sail is similarly supported with even more lifts. The mast is braced against stern winds by a number of stays while there is only a single stay taken forward to a little bowsprit. This would seem to indicate a quite light rig again, not intended for use except down wind in anything other than very light airs. The steering is also interesting for a single steering oar is shown lashed to the stern on the centreline making it the first known rudder. The steering oar was also supported by a lashing to a small vertical post like a mizzen mast, leaving it free to be turned as required by a vertical tiller by the helmsman. The steering oar or oars which were then more normal can be used to paddle or part row a boat round to help her into a new and required course. The fitting of a fixed centreline rudder indicates either that the boat was unusually handy or, more likely, that she normally used her rowing crew for any great manoeuvring.

In 1480 BC in the XVIII dynasty, Queen Hatshepsut organised an expedition to Punt (thought to be somewhere in Somaliland) and the

This Egyptian fresco shows one of the boats of Queen Hatshepsut's journey to Punt. The event was recorded with some fine reliefs and frescos in 1480 BC. These ships seem to be a little more advanced and may have been constructed with some kind of keel, perhaps similar to those of East Africa and the Indian ocean today. This fresco, discovered at Deir-el-Bahari, shows details of the ship, with deck beams and more complex sail and rigging.

Below These drawings are from the expedition of Karl Richard Lepsius in 1842-45. The journey was from the Sudan to Syria. The ships returned with an extensive collection of casts, drawings and original antiquities and papyrii. Pictures 2 and 3 dated 2040-1780 BC. 1, 4, 5, 6, 1567-1080.

event was recorded with some fine and detailed reliefs which have been found at *Thebes*. The ships look a little more advanced and may indeed be constructed with some kind of keel following perhaps the current practice in the Indian ocean ships or the East African ships. Those shown are about 70 feet in length with a beam of about 18 feet and a depth of about 5 feet. In addition to a keel they appear to be fitted with deck beams projecting through the shipside and secured with a heavy sheer strake. The deck beams may be fitted to support the deck only but it is likely that they were fitted primarily to brace the topside construction in

addition to the heavy rope supports fitted in the then normal manner. The wide shallow squaresail is supported by a single pole mast with both fore-stays and backstays but still without shrouds. The upper and lower yards of the squaresail are each built from two spars lashed together and extensively supported by lifts. Although the upper yard only is shown fitted with braces for controlling the direction

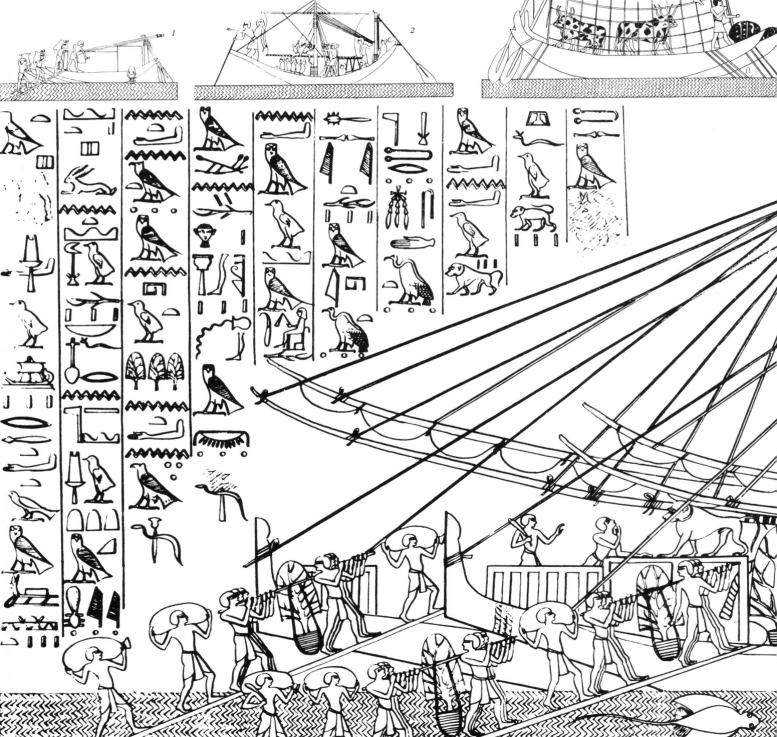

of the sail and no shrouds are fitted, the whole craft appears to be much more of a seagoing type. The spars look heavier and fenced platforms are fitted to both bow and stern.

Queen Hatshepsut also had ships built to carry large stone obelisks and it seems quite remarkable that these were no less than 195 feet in length and 70 feet in beam.

The model sailing ships recovered from the tomb of Tutenkhaman are rigged very much as those shown of the Punt expedition but with one small useful improvement. The steering oars are now carried by a transverse beam, a method which persisted right through Greek and Roman times until the steering oar was superceded by the rudder as we know it.

It is in the nature of man to fight and therefore it must have been as normal to fight your enemies afloat as it was to attack them on land. It is surprising therefore that the first representation of an actual sea battle is to be found in the tomb of Ramses III at *Medinet Habu* dating from about 1200 BC. These are actual warships for they have tops at the mastheads – little basket type platforms were fighting men could shower down the appropriate types of death and destruction on the enemy. As significant

Bottom *This illustration shows a further stage in the expedition to Punt. It shows the crew taking on board a cargo of incense and trees. The ships were constructed to carry much greater and heavier cargoes than previous discoveries would suggest had been attempted before.*

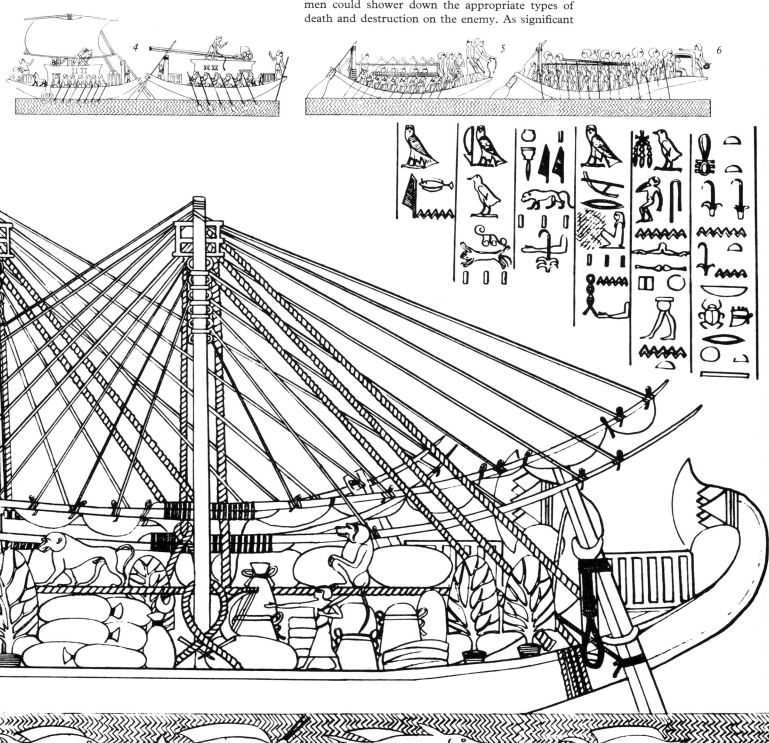

both for general seafaring and for sea wars the sails are fitted with a system of brails. This is a system of lines whereby the sail is furled to the yard which is then left aloft. The ship could therefore press into battle at full speed and then reduce sail without cluttering up the deck which was presumably packed with soldiers. This innovation is thought to have come from the northern Mediterranean and is part of the whole invention of the reefing sail. In fact the sail developed about this time with reefing lines to the yard at its head and a free foot became the universal sail of the Greeks and Romans.

The main line of sailing ship development then seems to have swung away from Egypt and to the

Greeks and Romans. In fact, a description by Herodotus in 400 BC of Egyptian trading craft speaks of vessels built of blocks of acacia as one would build a wall, caulked with papyrus, and pinned together with wooden pegs and all without ribs. An account which would have been valid a thousand years or more before.

This Egyptian fresco, from the tomb of Nakht, was discovered at Thebes and depicts further examples of the advances in boat building.

Below *The Portuguese conquered with a cross in one hand and a sword in the other. They were famous for their conquests in the Indian ocean. This early 16th century painting, by Cornelius Anthonissn, depicts Portuguese ships of war.*

Chapter II
The voyagers

Herodotus, born about 490 BC, reports that a hundred years or so earlier Africa was circumnavigated by the Phoenicians. The expedition was sent out by the Pharaoh Necho on the 15,000 mile voyage and returned via the Straits of Gibraltar, two or three years later. It was a long journey for sailors who probably tried at least to spend each night ashore and who even followed the natural rhythm of the seasons by staying ashore to grow crops along the way. As happens to travellers so often, on their return much of their account of their adventures was disbelieved. Herodotus himself, although he reports it, feels that it cannot be true that when they were at the southern tip of Afr the sun was to the north of them. This knowledge would only be available to a traveller who had penetrated well south of the equator and points out the unique nature of this early expedition, particularly as the Phoenicians did not have the compass. Very few other remarkable passages are recorded between this expedition and those of Bartolomeo Dias some two thousand years later.

We know, also from Herodotus, of the sad story of Sataspes of Samos who, in punishment for a crime, was sent by Xerxes to sail round Africa in an anticlockwise direction. The bulge of Africa proved too much for him and after meeting dwarfs clad in palm leaves at his furthest point south, he returned

Each maritime power, treasured its seafaring secrets

to face the alternative punishment which was impalement. We know from his account of Hanno of Carthage's remarkable colonizing voyage of about 500 BC. He was commissioned to found colonies and set out with sixty ships, each with fifty oars, filled with colonists, stores and equipment. He sailed through the Straits of Gibraltar and along the Moroccan coast, dropping off groups of colonists. From his account, it is possible to trace a journey which took him past Cape Verde to the Guinea coast. He describes his ships as pentecosters, fast 50 oared galleys which were principally used for sea raiding in packs. Their use rather than the use of the commodious merchantmen which would seem more natural for carrying all the goods required to establish colonies indicated perhaps that they were more frightened of the unknown dangers of the sea voyage than they were of the hardships ashore. His voyage was in fact of a summer's duration only and he returned when his supplies ran out.

Although there is little precise documentary evidence of great exploratory voyages for the next two thousand years, it does not mean of course that they did not occur. Historical knowledge, depending as it does on the accidents of documentary survival and other evidence, must inevitably be patchy. We can be fairly certain that voyaging did not stop for that would be unnatural, but it is certain that countries tended to regard information about trade routes and foreign ports, as important secrets of great commercial value. It is likely therefore that each new maritime power, Egyptian, Grecian, Roman, Arabian or Christian, treasured its own information and tended to disregard that of the previous regime. In the same way individual mariners were jealous of their geographical knowledge which represented the secrets of their own craft at a time when craftsmen in general hugged their trades tightly to them. It is unlikely, therefore, that seamen would lightly offer their knowledge to scholars, who might have recorded it for posterity. Thus, information was not recorded until spurred by the occasional far-seeing and powerful personality such as Ptolemy, Prince Henry the Navigator and Hakluyt, that any real pooling of knowledge of sea routes took place.

It is often quoted that Columbus' crew were frightened of falling over the edge of the world, which they believed to be a flat dish. It seems unlikely that seamen who must have been accustomed to the sight of ships and indeed land appearing and disappearing over the horizon would be serious about such a possibility; especially since Ptolemy of Alexander, who collated his famous treatise on geography about 150 AD, had shown the world to be round. There was a similar belief stretching as far back as to the days of the Babylonians. It is more likely that Columbus's men were making an early version of the standard seaman's joke about falling off the edge of the chart or getting caught in its fold.

The next outburst of exploratory voyaging of which we know occurred in the fifteenth century, principally based on the Portuguese exploration inspired by Prince Henry. At that time there was a reasonable basis of information about much of the world. Europe, the near east and the northern part of Africa were tolerably mapped and there was information on India and China, and even a tiny suspicion about the possibility of an America. There was still 'Terra Incognita' in plenty however, to be explored for booty, trade and even evangelizing.

Prince Henry set up at Sagres in the south west of Portugal a centre for the investigation and correlation of all seafaring knowledge: the ships, the seas they sailed upon, instruments and charts. More important, he made the knowledge collected accessible to all seafarers. He gathered round him the best navigators, cartographers, astrologers, shipbuilders, and seamen, and he despatched expeditions to fill in specific gaps in the information available. His explorers voyaged in the main along the west coast of Africa and to the Azores, Canaries and Cape Verde Islands. In addition to knowledge of local

1427, the discovery of the Azores, a turning point in navigation

conditions in each area they were also seeking a new sea route to India, avoiding the Arab dominated route down the Red Sea and across the Indian Ocean.

The discovery of the Azores by the Portuguese in 1427 marked a turning point in ocean navigation, for they are in a zone where variable winds meet the trade winds. The Portuguese in their caravels became confident in making long tacks out to sea, as they penetrated further and further south. On returning they would keep the trade winds on the beam until they reached the latitude of the Azores when they turned east and homewards in the prevailing westerlies.

Prince Henry sent out two or three expeditions every year but there was considerable reluctance to pass south of Cape Bojador, now called Cape Juby, for they believed, and who could blame them, that there the sea was boiling and the sun would turn a man black. Prince Henry specifically sent a nobleman, Gil Eanes, to round the Cape and so disprove this in 1434, and when another expedition a few

they proved to be the real basis for most of the fifteenth century exploration.

After Prince Henry the Navigator's death in 1460 his nephew King John II of Portugal continued with the search for a route round the south of Africa to the wealth of the Indies. In 1487 he sent out Bartolomeo Dias in a modest fleet of two caravels, each of about 100 tons, plus an additional storeship. Dioas managed to get well south towards the Cape, when he was caught in a strong northerly gale. By the time he had struggled back to land he

The development of shipping owes much to the Kings of Portugal

had passed the southern tip of Africa, which he feelingly named Cape Tempestuous. On his return to Lisbon, King John took a different view of the occasion and renamed it the Cape of Good Hope. In 1495, King Manual of Portugal too was obsessed with the trade routes to India and ordered Vasco da Gama to prepare another expedition. Dias himself designed two of the ships, the *Sao Gabriel* and the *Sao Raphael,* each of about 120 tons, altering the standard caravel model for the bad weather to be expected off the Cape. Illustrations of the period show them as being rigged with three masts, a single squaresail on the foremast, squaresail and square-topsail on the main, and a lateen mizzen. In fact the conventional ship rig of the day. Perhaps the modification was to apply the more easily handled ship rig, to the more easily driven caravel hull and this may have been one of the early steps in the development of the galleon. The other two ships were the small caravel *Berrio* and a large storeship.

Vasco da Gama set off in July 1497 and made first for the Cape Verde Islands. Then instead of the soul-destroying crawl down the African coast, among the baffling and changeable winds he set boldly off to sail well out into the Atlantic, on a route which was later proved ideal by the clipper ships. He took a broad sweep, arriving back at the African coast in November right into Table Bay. Then he punched the headwinds around the Cape and up the west coast all the way to Mombasa, before striking across the Indian Ocean to Calicut. The return journey was an ordeal of scurvy, and by the time he re-passed the Cape he had only two ships left and when he eventually returned to Lisbon after two years he had only 55 men left from the 170 who sailed with him. Vasco da Gama was piloted across the Indian Ocean by an Arab navigator and the Arabs had a well established trade with India. The Chinese also traded with India and East Africa, so in addition to establishing the Portuguese trade route to India, the expedition formed one of the first direct sea links between Europe and the Far East itself.

Christopher Columbus was one of the many fifteenth century seamen who dreamed of reaching the wealth of the Indies. After that route was proved and established, it became clear that there would be no further sponsorship from Portugal. Perhaps with Ptolemy's map, which had been re-published in

years later brought back gold and slaves, enthusiasm redoubled.

Gil Eanes sailed in a *barcos,* presumably a ship, and another voyager, Baldaia, in a *varinel,* and both are described as 'heavy vessels and difficult to manoeuvre, broad in the beam and lying low in the water.' The rig is not mentioned, but it is clear that these ships were not popular for this kind of work. Prince Henry promoted the use of the caravel for his explorations. It appears to have been used previously for transport around the coast of Portugal and as an offshore fishing boat. When he set up his school at Sagres, Henry deliberately chose a place as near as possible to Cape St. Vincent where 'the Mediterranean and the Great Ocean combat one another' and had unrivalled opportunities for

Caravels, beautiful and intriguing, the basis of 15th century exploration

selecting the best possible vessels to send out on his voyages. It was likely therefore, that they would start with the vessels they saw every day, coping well with the rough Atlantic seas.

The caravels they used were in fact, improved versions, increased in length, tonnage and in sails. They were rigged with two and later three lateen sails, set with the largest forward and in decreasing order of size aft, to give one of the most efficient windward working rigs ever devised. Not only was each sail of beautiful aerodynamic form, but the grouping gave a double slot effect which increases the the efficiency quite remarkably, an effect reinvented by Handley Page and other aircraft pioneers, nearly five hundred years later. These beautiful and intriguing ships can only be found by reference in old manuscripts and the occasional thumbnail drawing on a chart or rather indistinct picture, but

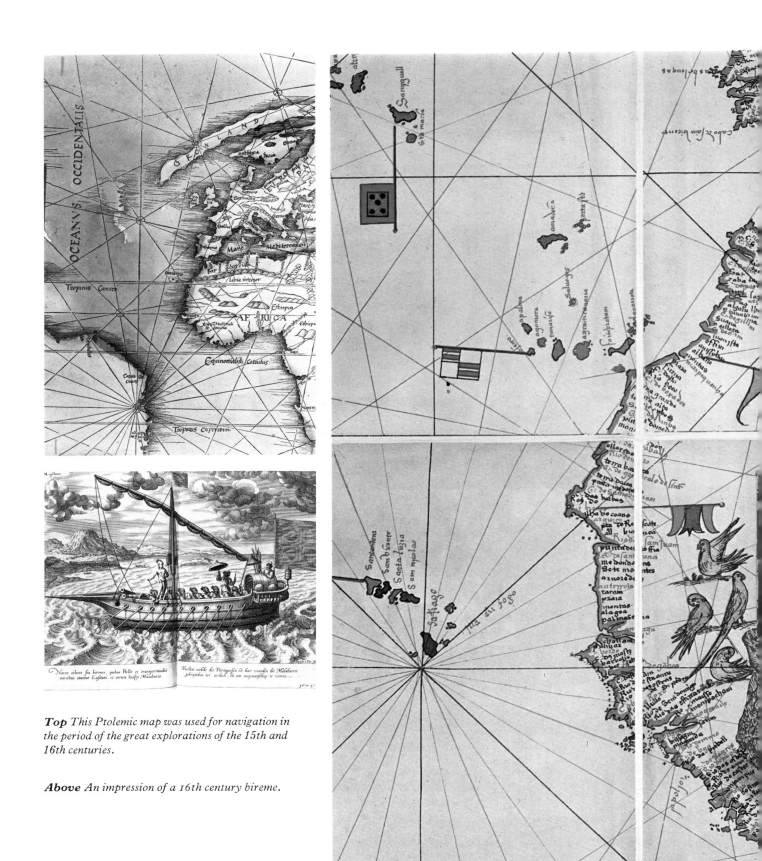

Top *This Ptolemic map was used for navigation in the period of the great explorations of the 15th and 16th centuries.*

Above *An impression of a 16th century bireme.*

Right *A detail of the Cantino map of 1502 showing the Portuguese fort of San Jorge de Mina, on the Guinea coast, which was once visited by Columbus.*

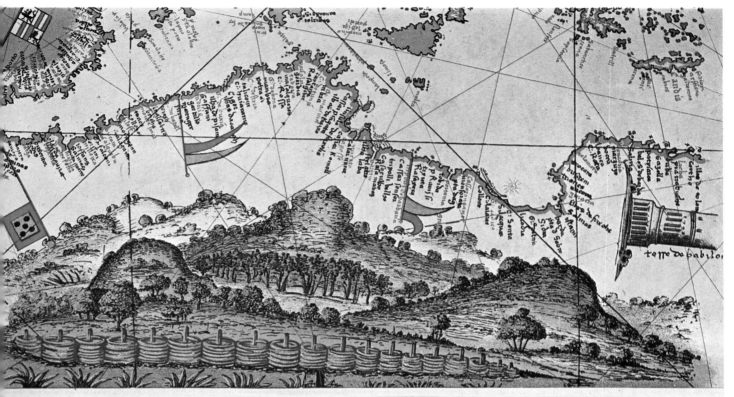

Os montes claros em affrica:

terra dell Rey organo o qual
Rey he muy nobre muito Rico

terra dell Rey de nubia o qual
Rey sempre tince continuada
mente guerra conel prestesoJua
o qual Rey he monzo xenupto
ap emigno de xristios

Serra lioa.

e ia esta serra lioa a muito ouxe este
he o mus fino que ay em nahua
parte xtraentom ga portugaill z mitos
escraba deles sam todes of zdole 9 be
mandinga 1 de capa z estes
tus mui
boas 2
yanos
dalgo
da

Castello damina.

a sotente principe doni manuell Rey de portugall cada anno doze cara
belas cam ouxes traze cada cara bro bria co ontra xvb nill pesos
douro val cada no pesso quinhentos ji elas vimeis traem unityos
eszbos z p timeira ta xo diz tra a com ses o muyto
pzoueita

tonre de babylon

23

Right *This illustration shows a map of the world after 1492. It is interesting in that it shows the South Pole at the top.*

Far right *A contemporary picture of Columbus taking observations of the sun.*

Centre *A portrait of Christopher Columbus by an unknown artist. Columbus made many voyages of exploration though he is most famous for his discovery of America.*

Right *One of Columbus' ships drawn from a contemporary woodcut.*

CRISTO: COLOMBO

1477, he turned his attention to Spain and to the possibilities of a westard route to the Indies. In 1492 he set off on his voyage with three ships, the ship rigged *Santa Maria* and the caravels *Nina* and *Pinta*, and more or less found America across his path. Whether his discovery of the continent is pre-dated by Lief Ericsson in Viking times, or by his contemporary Amerigo Vespucci is not really important. Columbus set off without prior knowledge of this enormous barrier between him and his goal.

Christopher Columbus, unhappy with his ships, discovered America

Experts seem to be agreed, that the Santa Maria was a small carrack, probably only about 80 feet in length, with a beam of about 26 feet, carrying a total sail area of about 3,500 square feet. Small as this ship appears to have been, Columbus felt that she had been forced on him against his will. He apparently thought that she was too slow and diffi-cult to manoeuvre and of too deep a draught to explore unknown coastlines. At any rate she was soon lost after her arrival and her leaky but immortal timbers used for building a fort. His other two ships were small caravels. The Pinta, is said to have been about 50 tons and the Nina rather less. The Pinta, incidentally, had her lateen sails replaced with squaresails in the Canary Islands and, there is no doubt that for a downwind trade wind passage from the Canaries to the West Indies, the squaresail is a much better rig than a lateen. The Pinta and the Nina arrived safely back home independently. For his next expedition, when he could choose his fleet, Columbus set off with no less than fourteen caravels and only three carracks. To his death, he thought that he had found a new corner of the Indies rather than a new continent. The Pope in recognition of the eastward influence of the Portuguese and the west-ward influence brought to the Spanish by Columbus, promptly divided the world between them, either as outright titles to new lands, or at least as uncon-tested semi-spheres of influence.

In 1519 Magellan was sent to make good the Spanish claim to the West. Charles V gave him a fleet of five ships of which we know little except their names and tonnages – *Santo Antonio*, 120 tons, *Trinidad*, 110 tons, *Concepcion*, 90 tons, *Victoria*, 85 tons, and *Santiago*, 75 tons. It is likely that they were three masted galleons. Magellan had under-taken to find a way past the barrier of America so that the Spanish could get at the Spice Islands of the Moluccas which they coveted. His voyage was beset with problems, a mutiny, a ship wreck, and a ship desertion, all before he had navigated the extremely difficult Straits named after him and found his way into the Pacific. Then, unprepared for the vastness of the Pacific, they suffered enor-mous privations during the four month voyage, which brought them to the Phillipines, where Magellan himself was killed in a fracas with the natives. It is ironic that the first man to round the world was in fact Magellan's Moluccan slave, who achieved this record when the fleet reached his

native islands. It is equally ironic that the sole ship of the five which left Spain to return to Seville, was the *Victoria* under the command of one of the mutineers, Sebastian del Cano.

Magellan became famous as the first man to sail across the Pacific but undoubtedly the ocean was already well known and used by the Chinese, and even the colonizers among the Polynesian islanders. It is a natural tendency for us to view exploration entirely from our own point of view.

The English were not involved with this partition of new lands, since the discoveries coincided with Henry VIII's divorce from Catherine of Aragon and his consequent dispute with the Pope. Francis Drake, determined to acquire both booty and demonstrate the practical precariousness of the Spanish claim to the Pacific, set sail in 1577. Like Magellan, Drake started out with five ships, although in general they were much smaller. The flagship was the *Pelican,* later renamed the *Golden Hind.* No accurate dimensions are known for her but because of her fame, the ship was preserved for a hundred years in a dry dock at Deptford on her return and her size can be guessed from that of the dock. This gives her a length overall of about 75 feet to the tip of her beakhead and about 60 feet stem to sternpost. Her beam must have been about 19 feet and her depth in the hold around nine to ten feet, but all these dimensions are extremely arguable. The other ships in the little fleet were the *Elizabeth*, 80 tons, *Marigold*, 30 tons, *Swan*, 50 tons, and a pinnace, the *Benedict*, of 15 tons, which was later changed for a 40 ton ship they captured off the coast of Africa.

Like Magellan, Drake had to deal with mutiny, disaffection and the general frittering away of his fleet. A storm drove him south in sight of Cape Horn and proved that there was yet another route into the Pacific. His attacks on the Spaniards in the Pacific, however, were extremely successful and he was also able to keep his crew much healthier than Magellan. He sailed as far north as Vancouver, stopped for a while in California and then decided to sail back via the East Indies and the Cape of Good Hope. Finally he returned to England, with fame and with a fortune, at the end of 1580.

Whereas the fifteenth century had its Dias, da Gama and Columbus, and the sixteenth its Magellan and Drake to mark out and girdle the world, the seventeenth century produced fewer and less illustrious names. It was more a time for filling in the details of the map, and above all for opening up new trading regions. The first half really belongs to the Dutch East India company, which was founded in 1602 and rapidly became the most powerful force

The Dutch East India company gave its name to merchantmen

in the Malay archipeligo. This company was to keep a very tight hold on the area, holding secret their charting, surveying and exploring. Their ships represented their general martial methods of colonization and were very similar to the ships built for the Dutch navy. Three masted galleons with at least one row of guns, probably rigged with three squaresails each on the forward mast and main and a square topsail over a lateen on the mizzen, were typical of the ships they used. A spritsail would be set at the end of the bowsprit with possibly a sprit topsail set over it in the slightly unlikely style of the period.

One of the governors of the company, Anthony van Diemen, sent Abel Tasman on a voyage of exploration in 1642. His avowed object was simply that of 'finding the remaining unknown parts of the terrestrial globe.' With two ships, the *Heemskerck* and the *Zeehaen,* they circumnavigated Australia and thereby proved that it was an independent continent. They also looked at New Zealand but did not discover that it was in fact in two parts, nor did they discover the legendary southern continent for which they had been keeping one eye open. After that it was left to the buccaneers and privateers to explore **and** open up the sea lanes around the Pacific and William Dampier in particular left interesting journals of his navigations.

Left top The straits of Magellan were originally shown by map makers to be an open passage, when in fact they were narrow and twisting, as later exploration showed.

Left below A 16th century artist's impression of a sailing ship.

Centre This ship of only 85 tons was the first to sail around the world. One of Ferdinand Magellan's fleet of five it set sail in September 1519 and returned to Spain three years later.

Below A fleet of canoes which rowed out to meet Magellan's fleet in the Philippines.

Right Sir Francis Drake, the famous English explorer set sail in 1577. He started out with five ships and sailed as far north as Vancouver, stopped for a while in California and then decided to sail back via the East Indies and the Cape of Good Hope. He returned to England in 1580.

Science and trade had become by the eighteenth century, the twin inspirations of the civilized world and this prompted further official and more detailed exploration with the British Admiralty, for one, providing men, money and ships. The search for the semi-mythical southern continent continued and when Cook was ordered to the Pacific to take scientists to Tahiti, to observe the transit of Venus. His further orders were to go south to look for the elusive south land. Comparatively few explorers are actually allowed to choose their craft, most having to take what their sponsors will spare. Cook however was given a free hand and it is hardly surprising that he should select a Whitby collier, since he was a Yorkshireman who first went to sea in that class of ship. His choice fell on a simple little collier called the *Earl of Pembroke*. She was slightly rebuilt

voyage to achieve accurate enough timing for calculations of longitude. Accurate timing such as this had been a dream of seamen ever since astronomical observations started to be used for sea navigation.

Cook's final voyage, again in the *Resolution*, but this time accompanied by the *Discovery*, took him first to the south and then north to the Bering sea and Alaska in search of the northwest passage. He returned to the Hawaiian Islands where he was killed by natives. *Resolution* and *Discovery* returned to England in 1780.

In the nineteenth century exploration was less on a global scale and grew even more scientific. It concentrated on the extension and the cataloguing of existing knowledge and surveying and charting of the remoter areas, the Poles, and the northwest passage, and a growing interest in marine biology.

Cooke, in his ship the Endeavour Bark charted the South Pacific

for the voyage and was renamed *Endeavour Bark* to avoid confusion with an *Endeavour* already on the navy list. Her plans are preserved from the Admiralty draughts for the alterations. She was built in 1764 and she was therefore only four years old when she was bought for Cook and was in every way a typical bluff, bowed, extremely simple, three masted vessel without the grace of a figurehead or beakhead or other decoration. She was somewhere about 100 feet in length with 30 feet beam and with 11 feet depth of hold. She is described as a cat-built bark, implying that she had full waterlines at the stern tapering off into a comparatively narrow transom at deck level.

Cook did not in fact find any new continents, but the detailed surveying and chart work that he did, of lands and places only touched upon by previous explorers, is classic and still in use. He circumnavigated New Zealand and charted the east coast of Australia. He was nearly wrecked off Queensland on a coral reef and discovered the Great Barrier Reef before sailing for home in 1771.

Still the great southern continent was not discovered and the Admiralty sent him off again the following year. This time he had two ships, the *Resolution* and the *Adventure*. Again he chose Whitby colliers which were purchased by the Admiralty and altered slightly for his use. The *Resolution* emerged with a figurehead and a proper stern cabin for the commander, looking more like a warship, but the *Adventure* remained a true collier bark. This second voyage was perhaps the most remarkable. In 1773 they crossed the Antartic circle, the first ships ever known to have done so. The ships were later separated and Cook made several forays into southern waters, rediscovering South Georgia and discovering several other islands. In 1775 Cook returned home after sailing 60,000 miles and, a most notable achievement for the time, having lost not a single crew member from scurvy. Throughout this voyage, he also used a chronometer to make precisely timed observations, thereby establishing that it was possible on a long

Quem timuit saevis etiam Neptunus in undis Et rediit toto victor ab Oceano Foedifragos bellis pelago, perstrauit Iberos DRAKIVS huic tumulus, aequoris unda fuit.

There was also a commercial urge to open up new markets in a time of comparative peace and affluence and to give occupation for the naval officers, men and ships, previously engaged in the European wars. Later the need to survey routes for the new signalling telegraph cables across the sea beds added another dimension to the explorations.

In 1818 four small whaling ships set off on explorations to the north. They were not particularly successful but they carried between them men who were to become renowned polar explorers. The *Trent* and the *Dorothea* were bound for Spitzbergen and towards the North Pole, commanded by John Franklin. The *Isabella* and the *Alexander* were bound to look for the northwest passage around the top of the American continent. The *Isabella* was commanded by John Ross with his nephew James Clark Ross as a midshipman on

board. The *Alexander* was commanded by William Parry. The *Isabella,* incidentally, later saved the Rosses and their men after they had spent four winters in the Arctic and lost their own ship, the *Victory* an 85 ton steam packet, in the ice, following their discovery of the north magnetic pole.

The following year, 1819, Parry set off with two new ships, the *Hecla* and the *Griper,* with James Clark Ross serving with him, again for the northwest passage. Although they failed to find it, they penetrated further west than anyone before. Further expeditions in 1821 and 1824 did no better. In 1827 Parry set off, again with James Clark Ross in the crew, in *Hecla* towards the North Pole. *Hecla* was left at Spitzbergen and Parry and Ross set out in two specially converted ship's boats, *Enterprise* and *Endeavour,* flat bottomed to resist ice pressure and fitted with metal runners to go over the ice. Unfortunately man-handling these two ton craft over broken ice proved much more difficult than they expected and to crown it all, they found that the ice itself was drifting in a strong southerly current and had to abandon their gallant attempt. Expeditions of this nature, which might be labelled failures in their avowed intention, nevertheless brought back information on hundreds of miles of new territory, very often fully charted and described.

With the arrival of iron ships, an urgent need had arisen to investigate the earth's magnetism, to ensure the accuracy of the more delicate compasses which were required. Among other expeditions the British Admiralty despatched Captain James Clark Ross with *HMS Terror* of 340 tons and *HMS*

Erebus of 370 tons to find and plot the south magnetic pole. Both ships had been bomb ketches and were very heavily built to withstand the shock of firing big guns. They were further strengthened for the ice and Ross, from his previous experience of arctic work, is said to have had the provisions stowed so as to form a solid mass inside the holds. Bomb ketches were never designed for handy sailing, although their great beam allowed them to carry all plain sail in half a gale of wind. Their bluff bows and coarse lines made them both slow and difficult to steer. In their four year expedition, they took numerous observations while they explored the Antarctic in general. They discovered and named Victoria Land, the Ross Sea, Mount Erebus, Mount Terror, and the Ross Ice Barrier.

Erebus and Terror were later fitted with steam engines and took Sir John Franklin on his last and ill-fated expedition to look for the northwest passage in 1845. None of the 129 men survived and the two vessels disappeared completely, except for a mysterious sighting on an early morning in April 1851, when the English brig *Renovation* met an iceflow off the Newfoundland Banks, carrying with it two three-masted ships whose description fitted Erebus and Terror.

In 1831 a 90 foot three master, *HMS Beagle,* classed as a 10 gun brig of 242 tons, left Plymouth on what was a more or less routine voyage. Its mission was to chart some more of the South American coast and to carry out a chain of chronological reckonings right around the world. It is significant of the general interest in science at this time, that it was not thought very remarkable to

Above Botany Bay at the time of Cook's exploration. He chose Whitby colliers as his ships, which were bought by the Admiralty, and altered for his use.

include a naturalist and an artist in the crew of 74, to report and note anything of interest they might come across on the voyage. The Beagle voyage is notable because the naturalist was Charles Darwin who, despite sea-sickness, kept a passionate and close interest in everything he saw over the whole five years he was away. It is also indicative of the standards of accurate timing required by the voyage that the Beagle carried not less than 22 chronometers all packed away with great care in beds of sawdust.

The new dimension in exploration was the depth of the ocean and the voyage of the *Challenger* in

1872/76 brought its importance to public attention. It was inspired principally by the work of *HMS Lightning* and *HMS Porcupine* when surveying routes for the new submarine cables. The depths and conditions recorded in these surveys astonished the scientists of the day, and the Royal Society resolved on a major expedition of about four years duration, so that the sea bed could be methodically explored. The Admiralty offered HMS Challenger, a wooden three masted ship with a 1234 horsepower engine driving a single propeller. She was of a class known as a steam corvette and had a displacement of 2306 tons and was about fourteen years old at the time of the expedition. All but two of her 64 pounder main deck guns were removed and she was extensively rebuilt with a laboratory, dark room, aquarium, and large chart room, together with cabins for the many scientists.

In her three-and-a-half-year voyage she travelled over 68,000 miles, sailing part of the time and using her engine at others and when trawling, dredging, or taking soundings. She collected mineral as well as botanical and zoological specimens and made extensive deep sea soundings, temperature readings and analyses of the chemical composition of seawater samples. She not only laid the basis for the present science of oceanography but she collected so much data that it is still being studied today.

Left An impression dated about 1900, of *HMS Beagle*. She was a 90 foot three master, classed as a ten gun brig of 242 tons.

Below HMS Challenger, a wooden three master with a 1234 horsepower engine, driving a single propeller. She was a steam corvette.

Below This 19th century print depicts the departure
of the Honourable East India Company's ship Inglis,
from St. Helena in company with other vessels.

Chapter III
The traders and the clippers

The ordinary everyday merchantman usually gets scant attention from the artists and the chroniclers, especially if there is some dramatic contest such as a war going on. This helps make it difficult for us to realize the considerable number of ships that were in daily use in the sixteenth and seventeenth centuries. At the beginning of the seventeenth, however, it is recorded that the Dutch, the dominant sea trading nation of the time, had over ten thousand ships, manned by a hundred thousand or so seamen.

The principal ship type was the *fluyt*, a rather flat bottomed, narrow ship with a rounded stern. Apparently the early craft of the type were heavily influenced by the prevailing method of assessing

Above *An advertisment of 1609 for emigrant ships shows the great increase in social mobility during the 17th century which was brought about by the developments in sail. This example offers most excellent opportunities for planting in Virginia.*

Above right *A 17th century oil painting of a Dutch East Indiaman, near the shore. The merchant ships rapidly became streamlined for a quick safe passage to the Indies.*

Right *Dutch East Indiaman about to engage in battle. Since they had to fight off pirates and were occasionally used in the colonial wars, the ships were very similar to naval frigates in construction.*

tonnage for dues and were excessively narrow on the deck. A new system of measurement became current about 1669 and later ships were less exaggerated. It seems that later the *fluyt* developed into the *pink,* still showing the rounded stern, but with a stern castle projection which was greatly narrowed (possibly pinked) in at the after end. A *pinnace* was thought to be a smaller version of the *fluyt,* but with a transom rather than a planked stern. The *fluyt* was apparently rigged, with three masts with squaresails and topsails on both the forward masts and a lateen mizzen. Topgallants

Merchantmen were armed like warships throughout the 18th century

were occasionally fitted but they were normally omitted to make the ships easier to handle, a desirable factor with the general shortage of seamen for such a large Dutch fleet.

In fact all manner of rigs are to be seen in contemporary illustrations. At the time ships were more commonly categorized by their hull type, or the use to which they were put, rather than by their rigs. Identification by rig came later, probably with the vast increase in ocean going which took place in the nineteenth century. When the hull is over the horizon, it makes better sense to recognize a ship by the sail plan which is visible. Names like *polacca* and *barque* turn up in contemporary documents. *Polacca* is generally meant to imply that the ship is rigged with pole masts in one piece rather than in separate lower, topmasts and topgallant masts, which were necessary in the bigger ships and warships. *Barque,* however, seems to mean quite different things to different writers and is not necessarily connected with the barque rig of the clipper ship times.

The Swedish master shipwright Chapman, in a book published in 1768, divides merchant ships into five types: the *frigate* which was flat sterned, the *hagboat* where the stern planking continued up to the taffrail at the top of the hull, the *pink* with its rounded and narrowed stern, the *cat* and the *barque.* The first three groups were fitted with beakheads, the latter two were not.

Throughout the eighteenth century the majority of merchantmen were armed. Thus they looked very like warships except that on closer inspection it could be seen that they carried fewer guns, or guns of lesser power. The normal rig was that of the frigate, but some owners refused to fit topgallants, whereas others gave their ships the full outfit up to and including royals.

The original *East Indiamen* were small roomy vessels probably of the pinnace type but rigged and fitted out in a manner very similar to naval frigates. This was as a result of both fear of pirates on their route to the Indies and of their occasional employment in colonial wars. Throughout the life of the East India companies, the size of their ships grew. Chapman, for instance, shows a ship of 676 tons pierced for 28 guns and obviously based on the 32 gun class frigates. By the end of the century the East Indiamen were 1,200 tonners, based largely

Right *This 19th century painting shows shipping in the Thames estuary.*

Opposite *The Old Custom House Quay, shown in this painting by Samuel Scott (1702-1772). Pictured are mid-18th century vessels.*

on 64 gun warships, although with a need for greater cargo volume they had flatter floors and fuller bilges. Steel's 'Naval Architecture' of 1804 details a 1,257 ton East Indiaman which again is very like a large sailing warship to the casual observer but with important differences on closer inspection. The upper deck is continuous, with a very flat sheer, the shipsides are wall-like and without the tumblehome of the warship and the bilges are fuller for cargo capacity. Most important however the bottom row of gunports are just painted on the outside and the lower deck is not pierced at all for guns. By 1815 high bulwarks were fitted from end to end and the

Of a fleet of 200 coasters, 140 were wrecked off the Norfolk Coast

East Indiamen lost all appearance of the gracefully curved sheer which had been a mark of the sailing ship since the time of reed rafts.

Throughout their joint history, the *West Indiaman* was always a very much smaller ship than the East Indiaman, scarcely reaching 800 tons in size and usually nearer 500. Although the West Indiaman carried guns and were rigged along warship lines, they looked very different. In place of the rather smooth profile of the warship and contemporary merchant ship, they showed a very irregular outline with as many as four different deck levels. For some reason they followed the Elizabethan builder in putting headroom below decks, were it suited the accommodation requirements rather than the other way around. Such a vessel might have eight guns a side, but these would appear through the shipside on four different levels. Eventually, the West Indiaman was tidied up to look a bit more like a small frigate but never approached anything like the full line of battle majesty of the East Indiaman.

By this time the main trade routes were established around the world, with merchant ships sticking as far as possible to paths which gave them the maximum amount of fair wind sailing. In the Trade winds for instance, and the minimum of both head winds and calms. When it came to working into harbour, they would if there were any baffling breezes, sit tight until the wind changed, in their favour or, latterly, until a steam tug arrived. Small craft were never important enough for tugs and in Europe and North America had to work in tidal streams and currents which might equal their maximum sailing speeds. Windward performance therefore was of much greater moment to them than it was to the big ships. If it is difficult to grasp the sheer numbers of offshore craft, it is much more so to realise how many small craft there were or generally, how dangerous their work was. In 1692 one hundred and forty of a fleet of two hundred coasters were reported wrecked on the north Norfolk coast, together with fifty ships outward bound from the Wash. In 1755 a fleet of over two hundred coasters was reported putting out of Yarmouth Roads, for the north and running into trouble. In 1770 thirty vessels are reported cast up on Lowestoft sands, and so the reports can be read until this century.

Most of the small coasters probably were rigged with two masts and the name brigantine starts to be seen at the end of the seventeenth century for two masted vessels square rigged on both masts. When the name *brig* began to be commonly used for this rig, the definition of a *brigantine* became one of a square rig on the foremast and fore and aft rig on the mainmast. There were of course all manner of variations, including the snow rig where a third mast was set up immediately aft of the mainmast, specifically to let the gaff sail operate clear of all the gear on the mainmast. Basically it was a means of fitting a bigger gaff sail, or spanker as it was known in three masters, without altering the proportions of the brig rig.

The French channel fisherman developed from the time of the middle ages the lugsail rig, which is a square rig turned on its side to operate closely fore and aft. The French lugger often had three masts and fitted topsails over each lower sail and added a jib working on a long bowsprit for good measure. As a windward rig it is excellent although difficult or troublesome to tack. This rig emphasizes again the importance of windward ability to the small boat working in open water, which might have to make over the wind and tide to get home.

The gaff rigged cutter was generally used by the English and other European nations as a despatch and patrol vessel. The rig seems to have stemmed from the rig the Dutch used for their yachts, which were developed from small fast patrol craft. A gaff cutter of the eighteenth century would have a gaff

mainsail, a staysail and a jib or bowsprit staysail and would have a squaresail as a running sail. Some cutters used upper and lower square topsails and presented a very lofty appearance.

There is an apocryphal story, that when a small two masted vessel was launched at Gloucester, Massachusetts in 1713, she entered the water so gracefully that her owner was moved to comment on how well she 'schooned' thereby inventing the whole breed of *schooners*. Two masted fore and aft rigged craft had certainly been seen before, among the general array of rigs in Europe and possibly also in America. However, there is no doubt that the American schooner became a distinct and extremely successful type of craft in its own right. It may have been promoted by the generally offshore winds of the east coast of America, which put a premium on fast sailing with the wind abeam. The Admiralty in their careful way, recorded the lines

The American schooner became a successful ship in its own right

of an American schooner showing a craft with a distinct air of the caravel about her hull form and carrying a great deal of sail. She was two masted with gaff sails on each mast. The foremast is set well forward leaving no room for a staysail but she is fitted with two jibs on a long bowsprit and has square topsails on both masts.

In the 1830s, the fastest ships afloat were the *Blackwall frigates*. These ships were built on the Thames privately for charter to the East India Company but followed a very standardized form, so that they would be readily acceptable to the company. When their monopoly of the eastern trade was repealed in 1833, the way was open for improvements to be made. In 1838 the Blackwall yard built frigates which were without a poop and with only a single set of stern and quarter windows. A few years later the Smith yard on the Tyne launched a pair of ships, the *Marlborough* and the *Blenheim*, with completely flush decks.

Meanwhile the Americans had fully discovered the advantages of fast sailing ships, after successfully building ships for blockade running and privateering

Below *The Boston Tea Party. Unimpressed by the East India Company's desire to avoid bancruptcy by shipping surplus tea into America, patriotic Bostonians flung the chests into the harbour.*

38

during the 1812/4 War of Independence. The same ships were put to peaceful uses after the war and were found to be in great commercial demand. They were in equal demand by pirates, smugglers, and slavers on the one hand and by the navies who had to catch them on the other. Baltimore-built ships had an excellent reputation for their performance and this thriving demand helped to develop a long hulled fine, even hollow bowed, type of vessel, which became known as the *Baltimore clipper*.

The transatlantic trade in the 1820s was a fairly leisurely one in terms of speed. A typical immigrant ship from Europe would probably take forty days for the voyage, possible not a matter of great importance to the first class passengers accommodated in cabins in the poop, but appalling for the main bulk of the immigrants who were packed into the 'tween decks like sardines. This profitable trade was wide open to take over by steam and a regular steamship service was in operation by 1838. Wild competition between the steam packets and sailing clipper packets went on for years, with the sailing ships being driven harder and harder to keep up with the reliable timing of the steamships. The sailing ship still remained supreme for longer passages, where the problems of coaling limited her rivals but the pressure was on all the time to push up the

speed of these vital crossings.

By 1843 American shipbuilders had begun to apply thc lessons learned in the Baltimore brigs and schooners to larger ships. They had begun to design and produce large full rigged sailing ships of 750 tons with the same style of hull. The first real clipper ship, as we understand the term, was probably the *Rainbow* launched at New York in 1845. She was revolutionary of course, in her fine hull after two centuries of wide bowed ships, but most startling to the eye must have been her stark simplicity. Painted black without any of the gunports and very little indeed of the giltwork, she must have looked extremely fast and elegant and she certainly proved both fast and commercial. 1847 saw the discovery of gold in California and started an almost insatiable demand for passages from the east coast, for would-be gold diggers round the Horn to the goldfields. Ship owners could almost charge what they liked for passage in a fast ship and they could sign up as many crew as they needed, who were only too pleased to work their passages to California. The demand for fast vessels was intense and limited entirely to American ships by American law. The problem lay in the accummulation of ships on the west coast as their crews lit out for the goldfields. Fortunately, this problem practically

Above The famous race home from China, between the Ariel and the Taeping. They arrived home within hours of each other after 98 days at sea. The Ariel was built in 1865 by Steele and Sons at Greenock.

coincided with the repeal of British Navigation Acts which had limited British trade to British ships. The clippers could now embark a double crew, lose half of them to the gold rush, sail for China to load tea, and make a profitable voyage to London. The slower British ships which had been keeping the tea trade to themselves, found that they were quite outclassed for the valuable first tea crop and had to be content with the unprofitable follow-up cargoes.

There had not really been a great demand for fast ships for the British trade until this point. The British equivalent of the Baltimore clippers were

The wood shortage led to the introduction of iron and steel

the small fast schooners and brigs which were built in Scotland, principally in Aberdeen, for the Baltic trade and of which the *Scottish Maid* of 1839 is probably the first with real clipper potential. The British started building clippers following the Americans and had a long hard struggle to catch up. After the building of the enormous fleets of wooden ships which culminated in Trafalgar, there was something of a shortage of wood in England suitable for shipbuilding. Therefore, there was a great deal of experiment with iron components, particularly knees and frames.

European shipbuilders pressed ahead with iron in ship construction, whereas the Americans with great reserves of timber stuck to wood construction. Steam ships came quite quickly to iron plating, but it was thought by seamen that the copper sheathing which was used to protect wooden ships from the shipworm of tropical waters, was essential to reduce fouling during a long passage. Copper sheathing on an iron ship presents frightening electrolytic corrosion problems and therefore the early English clippers were built of composite construction. That is with iron, and later steel, framing but planked with wood and sheathed with copper. Towards the end of the century, all sailing ships were built in iron; even the masts and spars were built of iron tubes and wire rigging had almost completely superseded rope for the standing rigging.

The California trade for clippers effectively came to a close when a railway was laid across the Isthmus of Panama, with connecting steamer services on both sides. Just as the demand for fast passages to California was dropping off, however, the Victoria gold rush started in Australia in the 1850s. The Americans were ready with fast and suitable ships, whereas the British ships were overwhelmed with would-be passengers. The American ships had increased in size, to 1,800 tons, while most English ships were less than half that size. Further, the American ships had a reputation for fast passages, making Atlantic crossings in about fourteen days west to east and eighteen days east to west; less than half the time of the old immigrant ships. American ships were leased to British owners and more ships were commissioned from American yards. McKay built the *Lightning* for a British owner in 1854, the

first ship to be built in the United States for a British owner since the War of Independence. The Lightning was 244 feet in length, by 44 feet beam and 1,468 tons. She was built with two complete decks and a poop extended forward for additional accommodation. She carried four cabins aft for first class passengers, housed the second class in a deckhouse amidships with twelve cabins, and the immigrants below decks.

The lines of the tea clippers of the 1850s and 60s were derived principally from the American wooden clippers such as the *Lightning* and *Champion of the Seas*, both designed by McKay. They were built with a beam to length ratio of about 5·5. The fully developed tea clippers such as the *Cutty Sark* and the *Thermopylae* were even finer with a ratio of about 5·7. They were also of rather finer section, for they were intended for a trade where the sheer bulk of the cargo was secondary to speed. There was a very large premium on the first of each season's tea crop to reach London. The tea clippers were probably the fastest ships ever produced, for they consistently outran the wool clippers when they were diverted to that trade. The Cutty Sark and the Thermopylae averaged 85 day passages from Melbourne to London over a decade, with a best run of 71 days, whereas the average for the genuine wool clippers over the same route was 90 days.

The British steel, wool clippers were very successful and it was in answer to their challenge that the American clipper master builder McKay built his masterpiece the *Great Republic* of 4,555 tons, 325 feet in length and 55 feet in beam. This marvellous ship carried a great spread of sail, as she was originally designed with skysails over her royals and moonsails over her skysails. She was square rigged on three of her four masts and fore and aft rigged on the fourth and would these days have been called a barque. In such a vessel sail handling had again become a problem for a working trading ship which could not carry unlimited hands who worked the rig on board warships. McKay split the topsails in the Great Republic in a manner which became standard for all ships in a few years. Sadly this ship caught fire before her maiden voyage in 1853 and although rebuilt, she was too late for her planned market and was not ever successful.

The Cutty Sark and the Thermopylae epitomise the tea clippers. They were both within a few feet of the same dimensions, which may not have been accidental, since the Cutty Sark was built as a rival to the other. They were not, however, outstandingly fast among tea clippers, although they both shone in the wool trade. The famous *Ariel,* for instance, was built in 1865 by Steele & Sons' yard at Greenock, who had by now rivalled the work of the original British clipper yards of Aberdeen. Their speciality was ships with very fine lines aft, which gave them additional ability to ghost along in calm weather. The Ariel in particular was said to be able to get along at four knots, by the shaking of her sails when all around her had stopped dead in the water. It is perhaps this ability, as much as top speed which made for the successful clipper. The ability to steal through a calm to the next patch of wind, while your rival remained stuck in it could mean a large and profitable lead in a race to port. It was for this, as much as for speed with the wind blowing, that the clippers surrounded themselves with swathes of sail. The Ariel and the *Taeping* ran an epic race home from China one year, to arrive within hours of each other after 98 days. The Cutty Sark and the Thermopylae, although rated quite high as tea clippers never got within ten days of such a passage time.

The opening of the Suez Canal in 1869 effectively did for the tea clippers. Trade continued for a year or two, because the shippers thought that the tea would get home in better condition in wooden sailing ships rather than in iron steamers. When this did not prove to be the case, the 60 day passages via the canal by fast steamship were unbeatable and the tea clippers were put onto the Australian wool trade.

The later American wooden clippers were known as 'down easters', from the placing of the building yards of Maine, Massachusetts and Connecticut. They were built for capacity as much as for speed and were plainly constructed and finished without much decoration. The depression of 1868 effectively put an end to this construction and the very last wooden square rigger, the *Arvan*, was launched at Phippsburg in Maine in 1891.

Up until this time the average size of the wool clippers was about 2,000 tons but in the 1880s, in an attempt to increase efficiency and to keep costs down, they were built as large as 3,000 tons. At the same time, the use of iron construction had made the hulls some fifteen per cent lighter than wood and this gave additional cargo capacity. The wool clippers held their own in increasing competition until about 1890, when they were rebuilt and switched either to general cargoes or to the Chilean guano trade.

Somewhat forlorn attempts were made with even larger sailing ships to get the economics right and to make sailing ships pay again. In 1890 a steel five masted barque, the *France*, was launched from Hendersons yard in Glasgow for French owners. She was lost in 1901 but in 1902 the only five masted, full rigged ship ever built was launched. The *Preussen* was 407 feet long and 53 feet in beam. A second five masted barque, the *France II,* was built in France and launched at Rouen and was the largest sailing ship ever built. She was 8,000 tons, driven by a sail area of 68,350 square feet and was run by a crew of forty-five. She was, necessarily, fitted with every labour-saving device including two small auxiliary engines driving propellers. These were later removed and for a while the France II was a pure sailing vessel. During the first war, she was attacked by a German submarine, but escaped under a press of sail and with both motors running. She was lost in 1922 after going aground near the entrance to Noumea.

The American schooner builders also tried to get the economics right with increased size, for a time with success. Their answer was a large, simple hull propelled exclusively by fore and aft sails set on as many masts as necessary to get the required sail

Above *This illustration gives some idea of the scale of these ships. It shows men on the yardarm.*

Inset *Members of the crew of the famous tea clipper the Cutty Sark.*

43

area. Five and six masted schooners were common but the only seven masted schooner ever built was the *Thomas W. Lawson* in 1902. She was 395 feet in length, 50 feet beam, and with a depth of hold of 35 feet was claimed to have given the biggest cargo capacity ever carried by sail. It is interesting to compare her with the five masted square riggers, for in contrast to their forty-five man crews, the Thomas W. Lawson was run by a crew of sixteen. Unfortunately, after successful voyages off the American coast, she was sent across the Atlantic in 1907 and capsized off the Scillies. She was no beauty, but a brave attempt to keep sailing ships, in an increasingly mechanical age.

After the first world war, a number of sailing ships found employment in the Australian trade again but this time running wheat. It is sad to record that they were not so employed for their speed, or other advantages as ships, but because they were generally such a drug on the market that they could be kept as floating warehouses for their cargoes after they arrived. The commercial square rigger had effectively ended its days.

Steam had moved slowly at first into the maritime world. Seamen are probably more scared of fire at sea than of any other hazard. They took the utmost care over such matters as galley fires, which would be doused at the onset of any rough weather which might have rolled an ember or two onto the deck. To fit a roaring great boiler fire and a chimney, belching hot sparks into a wooden ship liberally coated with grease and tar, must have seemed the bad joke of all time. Further, to fill the cargo space with expensive coal for the ship's own boilers, rather than with paying cargo, must have looked like commercial suicide.

Steam power, actually produced successful propulsion for boats in the last quarter of the eighteenth century and was quickly accepted for such obvious

Above *The Sirius, a 100 ton steamer built for the Irish sea service. She was chartered in 1838 by the British and American Steam Navigation Company. The Sirius was one of the first steamers to be fitted with a surface condenser, instead of using salt water in the boilers.*

Right *The Savanah steamship. She was powered by paddle wheels.*

45

uses as harbour tugs. But it was a long time before steam was trusted on its own for work offshore. The first steam engined vessel to venture across an ocean in fact was the *American Savannah* in 1819, a fully rigged three master, which made occasional use of the engines. It was originally thought that the steam engine would form an auxiliary propulsion method for occasions when the wind did not serve, rather than the complete power unit it grew to be. The Savannah was powered by paddle wheels which, it is said, could be dismantled and stowed on deck in twenty minutes. Her modest smokestack had an elbow bend in it, so that it could be turned to improve the draught in the boiler.

The first Atlantic crossing with the steam engine working continuously the whole way, took place in 1838 when the 208 foot *Sirius* took 18 days and 10 hours between Cork and New York. Sirius was fitted with surface condensers, which allowed her boilers to be run all the way on fresh water, saving all the problems which had been found in attempting to use salt. The paddle steamer *Curacao* had previously actually steamed all the way from Rotterdam to Paramaribo in 28 days, but with frequent engine stops on the way for repairs to boilers and machinery. She was chiefly remarkable for her paddle wheels, which could be increased in diameter as the coal was used up and the ship floated lighter.

The strong mental division between the sailors and the engineers, is perhaps not surprising and persists up to the present day. The modern sailing yachtsman often resents the engine on which he relies for motoring to and from his moorings and there is a lack of real sympathy between the sailing men and the power cruisers. In the early days of steam, the seaman on deck clung to his masts and sails and even when his rig became much reduced persisted with high funnels, perhaps on the basis that if the worst came to the worst, a sail could be set on them. The engineers were just as blinkered, for their reports on early trials would often describe ship and engine in great detail and entirely ignore the lofty rig spread above them. Many of the pioneer craft were in fact delightful examples of what would be called motor sailers in these days. Patrick Miller's very early, twin hulled 25 foot steamer, was powered with a Symington atmospheric engine and had a two masted rig. It is recorded, that she made a good five knots under power, which would have been her speed under sail with a good breeze.

The building of iron ships, 'against nature' as it was to many seamen who could not see how they could float, must have been a great relief to seamen navigating the new steamships in continual fear of fire. The Atlantic is often taken as a proving ground for innovation and the legendary position of the *Great Britain,* the first screw propelled iron vessel to cross it, is not surprising. Designed by the master engineer of the day, Isambard Brunel, the 322 foot Great Britain was fitted with a thousand horsepower below decks, driving a six bladed, fifteen foot diameter propeller. Above decks, she had six rather short masts all fitted with gaff sails and best

described as schooner rigged, although she crossed square yards on two of them. Her first transatlantic voyage took under fifteen days at an average speed of over nine knots. She was very well built with six watertight compartments in her length and survived a year aground at Dundrum, use on the Australian run, conversion to sail, use as a hulk in the Falkland Islands and then neglect until she was recovered in 1970 and brought back to Bristol, where she was built, for restoration.

The general seafaring man's attitude to steam was however expressed by the Royal Yacht Squadron at a meeting in the Thatched House Tavern in 1827 in these terms:
'As a material object of this club is to promote seamanship and the improvements of sailing vessels, to

The beginnings of steam power were looked upon with distaste

which the application of steam engines is inimical, no vessel propelled by steam shall be admitted into the club and any member applying a steam engine to his yacht shall be disqualified thereby and cease to be a member'. Their attitude remained rigid until 1844 when the Squadron admitted yachts of more than 100 horsepower into membership, a view no doubt coloured by the building of the first Royal paddle steamer yacht, the *Victoria and Albert,* the year before.

The steam yacht then prospered and although most sailing men resisted the idea of putting machinery into their lovely craft, a good many appreciated the further freedom and seamanship of an auxiliary engine. Chief proponent of this approach was probably Lord Brassey, who had compound expansion engines of 350 indicated horsepower in his famous topsail schooner *Sunbeam.* In her he cruised great distances including a 37,000 mile, circumnavigation of the world. With her sails set, she looked like any of her sailing yacht contemporaries but when the wind dropped she could use her screw propeller to give her a speed of eight knots on four tons of coal a day.

This auxiliary engine approach looked attractive for the tea clippers and an experimental auxiliary steamer, the *Far East,* was built in the 60s. In order that her sailing performance should not be impaired the twin propellers could be lifted up into recesses in the stern. Whether this would have been a successful ship type or not is hard to say, for it was overtaken by the opening of the Suez Canal and the establishment of regular coaling depots all the way to China.

The ships of the conversion period from sail to steam were generally awkward looking craft and the auxiliary sail and the auxiliary engine sat together very uncomfortably. The problem was the sheer bulkiness of each power unit and although the principle of auxiliary propulsion was probably sound, there was not room on board for both. Now perhaps when powerful power units come in such very small packets we may see a revival of the auxiliary sailing ship.

Left This 19th century print shows the SS Great Britain in stormy seas. She was the first screw propelled iron vessel to cross the Atlantic.

Left The SS Great Britain, designed by Isambard Brunel was fitted with a 1000 horsepower engine below decks. She was recovered in 1970 and reconstructed in Bristol.

Chapter IV
Twentieth century sail

This picture shows the sail training ship Malcolm Miller, sister ship to the Sir Winston Churchill.

When the industrial revolution changed the face of the earth it also changed the face of the sea. It was said at the time that never again would we ever see the clouds of white sails which had embellished the scene for centuries. The coming of the steam engine and the internal combustion engine had replaced the seven thousand year old era of sail, with tall funnels belching smoke. Very few people at the start of this century could possibly have envisaged the scene today when there are probably more

Right *The Vasa, built in 1628. She had a displacement of 1300 tons, a beam of 37 feet and a draught of 16 feet. She also had 12,378 square feet of sail. This drawing is by Nils Stodberg.*

Far right *The SS Constitution during her reconstruction. She is now preserved in her building port of Boston, Massachusetts. She was built in 1797 as part of a fleet of six ships which were to form the basis of the US navy.*

Centre *The stern of the Vasa, from a drawing by Gunner Olofsen. The height is 65 feet and she has double galleries. In the upper part there are two large windows for the captain, between which there is a device showing two corn sheaves held by Cherubs, which are a symbol of her name. There is also a national coat of arms supported by lions.*

Right *The Vasa was excavated in the summer of 1961. Her decks were housed in an aluminium construction. This has the advantage of allowing for regulation of humidity to assist in preserving these remains.*

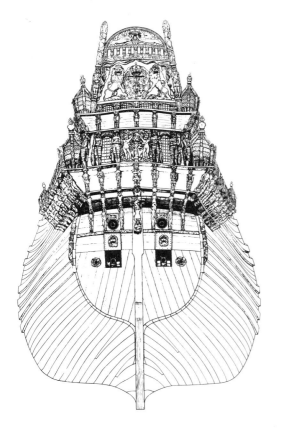

people in the world with actual practical experience under sail than ever before in history. As commercial sail faded, so began the day of the pleasure sailor and a surprising return to sail training for seamen bound for steamers. Another facet is the intense interest in the sailing ships of earlier generations. Relics are carefully dug out of bogs and painstakingly reconstructed and quite handsome sums of money are subscribed towards the preservation of notable sailing ships which have long since ended their commercial lives. Ships which were in fact of little interest in their day are often lovingly restored, even if otherwise fully documented, as if we cannot bear to lose a single extra specimen of the last of man's sailing heritage.

Many of the early relics are of great archaeological importance and it would not really be possible to be as certain of the details of early ships as we are without the physical presence in museums of such treasures as the ship from *Cheops'* pyramid, various remains from early Mediterranean shipwrecks, the *Nydam, Gokstad,* and *Oseberg* Viking ships, and the *Sutton Hoo* and *Graveney* remains. We now also have the *Bremen cog* in process of preservation to illuminate another dark period. Among the most impressive remains ever to have been brought up, as opposed to having been kept out of pride, is the ignominious wreck of the Swedish ship *Vasa.* Originally ordered by the King of Sweden in 1625 as part of his rapidly expanding fleet, this 230 foot by 38 foot three masted warship, displacing about 1,300 tons, keeled over and sank a few yards from the start of her maiden voyage in 1628. The disaster which drowned thirty of her crew was blamed on too fine a hull shape, which prevented the ballast being stowed low enough and on the lowest gun deck being too close to the waterline with the ports open when she heeled. Most of her main armament was salvaged at the time and she lay, probably thankfully forgotten by all concerned, until she was relocated and brought to the surface again in 1959. Now she is being most carefully looked after and scientifically treated to make her immortal as the sole representative of the many fine ships of the period.

The earliest existing ship which was not ever abandoned or taken out of service is *HMS Victory*,

The Victory, the oldest ship never to have been out of service

Nelson's flagship at Trafalgar and already an old ship at the time. Building of the Victory actually started in 1759 at Chatham, to the design of Sir Thomas Slade, senior surveyor at that time to the Royal Navy. With a hull length of 226 feet, she compares with the *Vasa* in length but has the much greater beam and may have displaced as much as 4,000 tons in full commission. During her life she was extensively rebuilt to keep her up to date and in the last few years she has had considerable parts of her structure replaced to keep her sound. Victory lay afloat in Portsmouth harbour for a hundred years before, in 1922, she was moved permanently into the world's oldest graving dock and was restored to her Trafalgar appearance.

Next in order of date are the American super frigates the *Constellation* and the *Constitution*, both now preserved in their building ports of Baltimore and Boston respectively. Both were built in 1797 as part of a fleet of six ships which were to form the basis of the US navy. They are both about 204 feet long with 43 feet of beam and are 2,200 tons. The design is said to have been inspired by the French *razées*, three-deckers cut down to single deckers, to make strong and steady, but rather slow, frigates. The Americans fined the hull lines as well and added the magic dimension of speed. The hull design was said to have been a great influence on the early Baltimore clippers.

Other ships of many types built since those days have been preserved. The brig *Niagra* which lies hauled out in Pennsylvania as a museum ship was built in 1812 and is famous for her association with Admiral Perry and his flag embroidered with 'Don't give up the ship'. The frigate *Trincomalee* built in Bombay in 1817 lies in Portsmouth Harbour as the training ship *Foudroyant* and a near sister ship, the *Unicorn*, laid down in 1794 but not completed until 1824 is a museum ship at Dundee. The whaler *Charles W. Morgan*, built in 1841, a full rigged three master, is preserved as a museum ship at Mystic Harbour Connecticut. She is painted with gunports in her original style, for she was built when it was necessary to deter pirates, and is fitted with the heavy wooden boat davits which distinguished a whaler. The *Star of India*, preserved at San Diego, is an iron ship built on the Isle of Man in 1863 as the full rigged ship *Euterpe*, hull length 216 feet,

beam 29 feet, and used for a very varied life which included running emigrants to Australia and supplying the Alaskan canneries. The *Balclutha*, built in 1886 in Glasgow, has come to rest as a museum ship in San Francisco after starting out in general trade and also finishing on the Alaskan cannery run.

Perhaps the most renowned of all the sailing ships of this period which has been kept for our wonder and enjoyment is the *Cutty Sark*. Built in Scotland of composite construction she was originally a tea clipper but really became famous for her contests with the *Thermopylae* on the Australian wool run. She frequently made record voyages and is said to have reached a speed of seventeen knots on many occasions. Now she is preserved in dry dock at Greenwich, fully rigged and showing off her 224 feet of severe elegance.

Then we have the ships made famous by the Arctic and Antarctic explorers and which have been preserved rather as monuments for their feats. The oldest of these is probably the *Fram*, built in 1892 for the famous Arctic expeditions of the Norwegian polar explorer, Nansen, for whom she was built. She was also used by Amundsen when he went to the South Pole in 1911 and therefore has the distinction of having gone further north and further south than any other ship. Fram was built of wood by the famous designer and builder Colin Archer at Reykavik in an extremely strong manner so as to be able to withstand ice pressure when frozen in. She is 117 feet in length by 36 feet beam and rigged as a three masted topsail schooner, and is about 400 tons.

The Fram and the Discovery, heroes of Arctic and Antarctic exploration

In London, the 171 foot *Discovery* lies alongside the Embankment. She was built at Dundee in 1901 on the lines of the Dundee whaler, especially for the British Royal Antarctic expedition of the same year, commanded by Scott. She was also used by the Hudson's Bay Company and for running arms to Russia in the World War I. Since her final voyage to the Antarctic in 1928-31, she has been used as a training ship and museum.

Two other little ships commemorate the last great exploration of the earth – the final threading of the north-west passage round the north of Canada. Amundsen's little *Gjoa* of 50 tons now lies in San Francisco. Between 1903 and 1906 this converted fishing sloop, with seven men on board, persisted between freeze-up and freeze-up, sailing gradually westward until finally she reached the Pacific. It was not until 1940 that the passage was made again, this time by the 104 foot auxiliary schooner *St. Roch* belonging to the Royal Canadian Mounted Police which started a two year voyage eastwards to Halifax, returning westwards in 1944. She is now preserved in a special building in Vancouver.

Another phenomenon of the current fantastic interest in sailing ships of earlier times is the building and sailing of full sized replicas or reconstructions. Some, of course, have been built specifically for film work but many more serious attempts at

Right The bow of HMS Victory, Nelson's famous flagship. She is now preserved in Portsmouth harbour. She was an old ship when she entered service for him.

authenticity are based between archaeological interest and national or institutional pride in past glories. The Scandinavians have made several Viking ship replicas and one was rowed across the Atlantic to add to the evidence for the Norsemen having discovered America long before Columbus. The *Santa Maria* herself has been the subject of reconstruction attempts but these have been based largely on estimates of what a normal nao of the period would have been like, for instance, there are no technical details available. A replica of the *Golden Hind* was built at Appledore and launched in 1973, once again as the result of intensive research into ships of the period, rather than from any exact information about the Golden Hind herself. Fortunately, however, there remains a little basic guidance from the recorded dimensions of the dock the actual ship was preserved in until she fell to pieces. The new *Golden Hinde* (as they prefer to spell it) is to make the voyage to San Francisco where she will become both a memorial to Drake's landing in the vicinity and a tourist attraction.

A few years earlier Hinks of Appledore, who built the Golden Hinde replica, completed another antique type of vessel to celebrate the third centenary of the founding of the Hudson's Bay Company. The original *Nonsuch* was built at Wivenhoe, Essex, and crossed to North America to trade with the Indians in 1668. On her return King Charles II gave a charter to a group of merchants to trade with the Hudson's Bay area. The new Nonsuch, as close

as possible, of course, to the original but based on fairly flimsy details, is a fine little square rigged ketch of 53 feet in length and with a beam of 15 feet 6 inches.

Other ships associated with the early days of American history have also been the subject of conjectural reconstructions. Full sized vessels, representing the ships which the Virginia company despatched with settlers to Jamestown in the winter of 1607 are now moored in Jamestown. These represent the *Susan Constant*, recorded as being 100 tons burden, the *Godspeed*, 40 tons burden, and the *Discovery*, 20 tons burden. The two larger ships are said to have been colliers before they were bought for the Virginia run and the Discovery was said to have been a pinnace more suitable for the coastal trade. The Discovery was thought to have been used subsequently for survey work on the American coast. Also that it was her charts which were used by the *Mayflower* on her historic arrival in 1620.

A replica of the Mayflower was also built, in Brixham in 1956, and in 1957 sailed for a commemorative voyage under the command of Alan Villiers to arrive at Plymouth, Massachussetts, where she is now a museum ship. The reconstruction, again built with the minimum of facts to go on, had a length of hull of 106 feet and a beam of 25 feet.

It is probably fair to comment, that many of these reconstructed vessels, of the time before building plans were kept or even made, are not all that

Below The Fram at the ice barrier during the South Pole expedition of 1910-1912. She was built in 1892 for the famous Arctic explorations of the Norwegian polar explorer Nansen and used by Amundsen in the 1911 expedition.

satisfactory. The mere absence of facts allows all manner of other considerations to creep into their design and construction. Some, for instance, have had to look like the craft shown in a modern painted reconstruction of the scene. Most have had to be adapted to become satisfactory museums, which means that headroom between decks has had to be increased. Most of them have had to be fitted with engines and made to meet current shipping regulations. Some, therefore, present a slightly uneasy

The history of sail is the basis of all modern seafaring

appearance to the eye. The reconstructions of later ships, on the other hand, can be more exactly based on the preserved plans and although liberties have to be taken in some areas they have probably been more satisfactory. The *Bounty II,* built for a film company in 1960, looks for instance a proper handsome little ship although to accommodate the film cameras and the twin engines she is at 133 feet in length no less than 30 feet longer than the original Bounty from whose lines she was built.

The two masted 130 foot schooner *America* laid British yachting by the heels in the famous race round the Isle of Wight in 1851. Ever since, the extraordinary and monumental series of match races for the America's Cup has kept her name in the public glare. It is not surprising that a replica of this famous ship should have been built in 1967 by Goudy and Stevens as a private yacht for the president of a brewing concern. What is slightly surprising is that the lines from which the replica was built were supplied by the British Admiralty, who had continued their good old practice and taken the lines off the original. Even such an historic and well documented craft has had to be slightly changed for the copy. The sheer has been raised six inches to improve the accommodation, the masts are less well raked, and a quarter of her ballast is now fitted outside rather than inside as in the original.

Possibly the latest ship to be subject for reconstruction in this manner, is the famous schooner *Bluenose,* champion of the international fishermen's races between the USA and Canada. Bluenose was built in 1921 especially for these contests and was lost in 1946 while trading to the West Indies. *Bluenose II* was built in 1963, to the same plans, in the same yard and modified only to give her proper charter accommodation for passengers and of course the inevitable twin engines.

Training in sailing ship handling has always been advocated by some seamen, as the only way to get a proper knowledge of the sea, wind and tide. The basis of seafaring which underlies all the modern miracle hardware of machinery and electronics with which the modern mariner is equipped. The advocates of sail training fought something of a rearguard action until about the last twenty years or so when suddenly the picture changed. Now there are sailing ships being built all over the world especially for the job and the Sail Training Associa-

Far left above A reproduction of Columbus' flagship, Santa Maria, under full sail.

Far left below RCMP schooner St Roch, built in 1928, was the first ship to navigate the North West passage from West to East and on completion of the return journey, to have made the voyages in both directions. She was a 300 ton ship and her captain was Staff Sergeant H A Larsen. She had a crew of eight and is now preserved in Vancouver Maritime Museum.

Left The Nonsuch under full sail, near Dawlish in Devon, on passage from Exeter to Brixham, on 21st August 1969. The original Nonsuch was built at Wivenhoe, Essex and crossed the Atlantic to North America to trade with the Indians in 1668.

tion races are better supported every year.

Many of the maritime nations of course, never stopped training under sail and, for instance, the Russians are reputed to run a large fleet from the great four masted bark *Krusenstern* of about 2,000 tons displacement, to modest schooners built especially for the purpose. They also took over the *Cristofero Colombo* as war reparations from the Italians, leaving them with her sister ship the *Amerigo Vespucci*. These are very large sailing ships, whose dimensions bear comparison with those of the *Victory* with a length of 269 feet, a beam of 51 feet, and of 4,000 tons displacement, although perhaps more on the lines of a frigate than a three decker. They both carry a crew of about 450 of whom a third are cadets.

Also part of the post-war redistribution was the German 1,800 ton steel bark the *Horst Wessel*. It took over from the *Danmark* as the US Coast Guard school ship and was re-named *Eagle*. Other close sisters of the Eagle are the Russian *Tovaristsch*, the Portuguese *Sagres II* and the current *Georg Fock II* of the German navy. Another ex-German sailing ship still in use, although dating from the

Far left Uphams shipyard Brixham, where the Mayflower II was constructed in 1956. She was massively timbered in the old fashion.

Left A fishing Schooner champion of the North American fishing fleet.

Below The Mayflower set out from Plymouth harbour in 1620 with 102 pilgrims on board and a crew of 20.

World War I reparations is the Polish *Dar Pormorza* which after service in France was sold to Poland in 1929.

The Danes run a 210 foot full rigged steel ship, the *Danmark*, built in 1933, borrowed by the American Coast Guard during the last war, and a smaller ship, also full rigged, the *Georg Stage* of 134 feet. Both take about 80 cadets to sea, in addition to the normal crew and instructors. The Norwegians had the full rigged 198 foot *Sorlandet* built in 1927 and have the 205 foot full rigged ship *Christian Radich*. The former took about 85 cadets and the latter takes about 100. The *Sorlandet* was also the last sail training ship to be built without an engine, although she is now fitted with a diesel. Another of the large and impressive sail training ships is the Spanish *Juan Sebastian de Elcano*, named after Magellan's old mutineer who completed the first circumnavigation of the world. She was built in 1927 and is 289 feet long, 3,750 tons displacement and is square rigged only on the forward of her four masts, making her a four masted topsail schooner.

These and many more represent sailing ships which, despite their current value for sail training are substantially relics of the sailing ship past. Even the smaller Swedish schooners the *Gladan* and *Falkan* are basically typical examples of commercial craft, which either have already or are now disappearing. The first of the latest breed of ships designed especially to give the experience of ship sailing, rather than to provide part of a training leading to a lifetime's profession of the sea, are probably the little Canadian brigantines *St. Lawrence* and *Pathfinder,* built in 1953 and 1963 respectively. These 60 footers were designed by Francis MacLachlan for the Canadian Sea Cadet corps and take 22 and 30 officers and crew respectively to sea, at a time. They are based at or near Toronto and are used mainly on the Great Lakes.

Although the Sail Training Association is principally a British organisation and the Tall Ships races the brainchild of that Association, it was not until 1966 that Britain had a sail training ship of her own. The *Sir Winston Churchill* launched in that year was followed by a sister ship, the *Malcolm Miller,* in 1968. These two three masted topsail schooners are 135 footers with about 26 foot beam and carry six permanent crew and 40 boys or girls. Since then the British Sea Cadets have built a 76 foot brig, *Royalist*, to take about 32 to sea and the Outward Bound Association has built a three masted schooner, the *Captain Scott*. Many other organizations are currently building ships along the same lines, using expensive outfits and labour intensive gear deliberately, for the pleasure and instruction they give. Many other youth training organisations, notably the Ocean Youth Club, are building modern yachts for the same purpose, but these are much less specialised and much more akin to the private yachts to be seen all around.

When the steamship took over the technical leadership afloat from the clipper and when iron construction superseded wood, two seven millen-

Right *The Royalist, training ship of the Sea Cadets.*